*25 best an   way to pop the
question that gets a "YES"*

Hannah A. Champor

Copyright © 2023 by Hannah A. Champor

All rights reserved. No part of this book may be reproduced or transmitted in any form or by any means, electronic or mechanical, including photocopying, recording, or by any information storage and retrieval system, without permission in writing from the copyright owner, except for brief quotations in critical reviews and articles.

Chapter 1: Recognizing the Signs of Readiness 5

    Timing is Everything: Understanding the Clues that She's Ready for the Next Step 8

    Identifying her emotional cues and subtle hints that indicate she may be ready for a proposal. 11

    Observing changes in the relationship dynamics that signal a deeper commitment. 14

    Communicating openly about future plans and goals to gauge her expectations. 17

Chapter 2: Finding the Perfect Moment 21

    Seizing the Moment: How to Discover the Ideal Time to Pop the Question" 25

    Recognizing milestone moments and shared accomplishments that signify the right time for a proposal 30

    Creating opportunities for memorable experiences to enhance the proposal setting. 33

    Leveraging special occasions and holidays to add magic and significance to the proposal 38

Chapter 3: Understanding Her Dream Proposal 40

    Fulfilling Her Wishes: Unraveling the Mystery of Her Dream Proposal 45

    Discovering her proposal fantasies through subtle inquiries and open conversations 49

    Analyzing her favorite romantic stories and movies to identify elements she desires in her proposal 53

    Paying attention to her reactions to others' proposals to discern her preferences 57

Chapter 4: Unconventional and Personalized Approaches 60

    Beyond Tradition: Crafting Unique and Personal Proposals She'll Never Forget 64

    Exploring non-traditional proposal ideas that align with her interests and passions 67

    .Incorporating shared hobbies, inside jokes, and cherished memories into the proposal plan 71

    Embracing creativity and thinking outside the box to make the proposal one-of-a-kind 74

Chapter 5: Enlisting Help and Making It Memorable 78

    The Power of Teamwork: Enlisting Support for a Heartwarming and Unforgettable Proposal..82

    Involving friends and family to create a surprise-filled proposal that showcases your love and support system..87

    Hiring professionals, such as photographers or musicians, to capture the moment and enhance the experience 91

    Incorporating small gestures of thoughtfulness to ensure the proposal is memorable and tailored to her preferences 95

25 of the best and most Creative way to pop the question 99

Conclusion: Embracing the Journey of Love 104

Chapter 1: Recognizing the Signs of Readiness

Timing is everything when it comes to proposing marriage to your partner. The key to a successful proposal is recognizing the signs of readiness, ensuring that both of you are on the same page and ready to take the next step in your relationship journey. By paying attention to subtle cues and openly communicating with your partner, you can confidently plan the perfect moment to pop the question.

One essential sign of readiness is emotional cues. Notice if your partner seems more emotionally connected and invested in the relationship. A willingness to discuss future plans, dreams, and aspirations can indicate a deeper commitment to the partnership. As you engage in heartfelt conversations about your future together, you can gain insight into her expectations and desires.

Shared accomplishments and milestone moments are also significant indicators. Celebrating achievements together, such as career advancements or personal growth, can strengthen your bond and signal that the relationship is progressing positively. These moments can create the ideal setting for a proposal, marking the culmination of your shared journey.

Open and honest communication is the backbone of any strong relationship. Initiating conversations about the topic of marriage without pressure or expectation can reveal your partner's thoughts on the matter. By creating a safe and supportive environment for discussing your feelings, you'll foster trust and openness between you both.

While recognizing the signs of readiness is vital, remember that every relationship is unique. It's crucial to respect your partner's timeline and not rush the process. If she's not yet ready for marriage, continue nurturing the bond and allowing the relationship to naturally evolve.

By being attuned to the emotional dynamics, celebrating shared achievements, and communicating openly, you can confidently gauge your partner's readiness for a proposal. Remember, the journey to marriage is one of mutual understanding and support. When the time is right, your heartfelt and sincere proposal will mark the beginning of a new and beautiful chapter in your love story.

Timing is Everything: Understanding the Clues that She's Ready for the Next Step

Embarking on the journey of proposing marriage is a momentous step in any relationship, and understanding the clues that indicate she's ready for the next chapter is crucial. By observing her actions, listening to her words, and connecting emotionally, you can confidently plan the perfect proposal that aligns with her desires and dreams.

One of the most significant clues that she's ready for the next step is an increased emotional connection. Notice if she seeks more quality time with you, expresses vulnerability, and shares her thoughts and feelings openly. These gestures demonstrate a growing sense of trust and intimacy, essential factors in a successful and fulfilling proposal.

As your relationship evolves, conversations about the future may naturally arise. If she initiates discussions about long-term plans, family, or shared goals, it could be a strong indicator of her readiness for marriage. Take these opportunities to express your own desires and actively listen to her perspective.

Her interest in wedding-related topics or marriage-centric media might also suggest her readiness. If she enthusiastically discusses wedding plans, admires engagement rings, or shares stories about friends' proposals, it's likely she's envisioning a future with you as her life partner.

Another vital clue is the level of support and involvement she seeks from you in various aspects of her life. If she actively involves you in decisions, values your opinion, and leans on you for support, it demonstrates her desire for a deeper commitment.

Ultimately, communication remains the foundation of any successful relationship. Engage in open and honest conversations about your feelings, intentions, and aspirations. Express your love and commitment, and encourage her to share her thoughts and dreams as well.

By understanding these clues and connecting with her on a deeper level, you'll gain valuable insight into her readiness for the next step. Remember that every relationship is unique, and the most meaningful proposals are those that reflect your mutual love and understanding. When the time is right, your thoughtful and heartfelt proposal will undoubtedly pave the way for a lifetime of happiness and love together.

Identifying her emotional cues and subtle hints that indicate she may be ready for a proposal.

In any relationship, emotional cues and subtle hints can provide valuable insights into your partner's readiness for the next step. Paying attention to her emotions and reactions can guide you towards planning a meaningful and heartfelt proposal that aligns with her desires.

One of the most significant emotional cues is a deepening sense of emotional intimacy. Notice if she becomes more vulnerable and open with you, sharing her hopes, fears, and dreams. A growing emotional connection can indicate that she feels secure and cherished in the relationship, laying the foundation for a potential proposal.

Her expressions of affection and appreciation may become more frequent and pronounced as she feels closer to you. Expressions of "I love you" and heartfelt compliments reveal her emotional investment in the relationship and her desire for a deeper commitment.

Consider her reactions to discussions about marriage or engagements, whether they are about friends or family members getting engaged or references to weddings in media. If she responds positively and seems excited or intrigued, it could suggest her readiness for a proposal.

Observe how she interacts with children or envisions her future family life. If she demonstrates a strong desire for starting a family or expresses enthusiasm about future parenting, it may indicate that she's thinking about building a life together.

Pay attention to any subtle hints she might drop about her ideal proposal or engagement ring. She may mention her favorite proposal stories or discuss elements she finds romantic or meaningful in a proposal. These hints can offer valuable guidance for crafting a personalized and special proposal.

Keep in mind that everyone communicates differently, and her emotional cues may be unique to her personality. The key is to listen actively, be attentive, and engage in open conversations about your future together. Understanding her emotional cues will not only help you identify her readiness for a proposal but also deepen your connection as a couple. When you're confident that the time is right, your thoughtful and attentive approach will undoubtedly lead to a proposal that reflects the depth of your love and commitment.

Observing changes in the relationship dynamics that signal a deeper commitment.

As a relationship evolves, subtle shifts in dynamics often indicate a deeper commitment and readiness for the next chapter. By keenly observing these changes, you can gain valuable insights into your partner's feelings and prepare for a meaningful proposal that aligns with the growth of your love.

One evident sign of a deeper commitment is an increased sense of partnership and mutual support. Notice if your partner starts seeking your advice or involving you in important decisions, both big and small. A desire to create a life together is often demonstrated by a willingness to work as a team, facing challenges and celebrating victories hand in hand.

Communication patterns may also change as the relationship becomes more serious. Observe if she becomes more open and comfortable discussing sensitive topics, future plans, and long-term aspirations. A willingness to share thoughts and feelings about the relationship indicates a sense of security and trust that lays a strong foundation for a potential proposal.

Another significant indicator of deeper commitment is the amount of time spent together. If your partner starts prioritizing quality time with you and actively making efforts to strengthen your bond, it shows her desire to nurture the relationship on a more profound level.

Take note of how your partner introduces you to others, especially to friends and family. If she includes you in important social circles and refers to you as "we" instead of "I" when discussing future plans, it suggests a shift towards a more committed and intertwined future.

Celebrate the moments of vulnerability and emotional growth in your relationship. If she becomes more comfortable sharing her fears and insecurities with you, it signifies a deepening of trust and emotional connection.

Remember, every relationship is unique, and changes in dynamics may manifest differently for different couples. The key is to be attentive, patient, and communicative in your observations. By keenly recognizing the shifts in relationship dynamics, you can confidently prepare for a proposal that reflects the profound love and commitment you both share. When the moment is right, your understanding and thoughtful approach will undoubtedly lead to a proposal that marks the beginning of a beautiful and cherished chapter in your love story.

Communicating openly about future plans and goals to gauge her expectations.

Asking the big question is a significant milestone in any relationship, and communicating openly about future plans and goals is essential to gauge your partner's expectations. Open dialogue fosters trust, strengthens your bond, and ensures that both of you are on the same page before taking the next step.

Initiate conversations about your future together, asking questions that invite your partner to share her aspirations and desires. Discuss your individual goals and dreams, as well as how you envision intertwining them as a couple. By encouraging an open and honest exchange, you create a safe space for both of you to express your hopes and expectations.

When discussing your future, pay attention to how she responds. Listen to the enthusiasm in her voice and the level of excitement she displays when sharing her vision. If she speaks passionately about building a life with you, it could indicate her readiness for a proposal.

Ask her what marriage means to her and how she envisions married life. Understanding her perspective will help you align your intentions and ensure that both of your expectations are compatible.

Be receptive to her concerns or fears about taking the next step. Some individuals may have reservations about marriage due to past experiences or uncertainties. Addressing these concerns with empathy and reassurance will demonstrate your commitment to understanding her feelings.

Remember that open communication goes beyond just verbal discussions. Observe her non-verbal cues, such as body language and expressions, during conversations about the future. These cues can provide valuable insights into her emotions and feelings about the subject.

Throughout your discussions, remain patient and supportive. Let her know that you value her thoughts and feelings, and that you're committed to working together as a team. Building a solid foundation of open communication and trust will pave the way for a more profound and meaningful proposal experience.

By communicating openly about future plans and goals, you create an environment where your partner feels safe to express her expectations and desires. Understanding her vision of the future will help you plan a proposal that reflects your shared dreams and celebrates the beautiful love you both share. With clarity and mutual understanding, your proposal will be an unforgettable moment that sets the stage for a lifetime of happiness together.

Chapter 2: Finding the Perfect Moment

Proposing marriage is a deeply significant moment in any relationship, and finding the perfect moment to pop the question adds an extra layer of magic and sentiment to the experience. By thoughtfully planning and recognizing opportune occasions, you can create an unforgettable proposal that will be cherished for a lifetime.

One essential consideration when finding the perfect moment is to align the proposal with shared milestones or significant events in your relationship. Whether it's celebrating an anniversary, a special date that holds sentimental value, or a shared accomplishment, tying the proposal to these moments adds depth and meaning to the experience.

Another opportunity to consider is during a romantic getaway or vacation. Traveling to a beautiful destination creates an enchanting backdrop for a proposal. Whether it's on a serene beach, a mountaintop, or amidst the charm of a foreign city, the new environment will heighten the emotional impact of the moment.

Take into account her preferences and interests when planning the proposal. If she loves nature, a proposal amidst a picturesque garden or during a scenic hike could be the perfect choice. For the art enthusiast, consider a proposal at an art gallery or museum, surrounded by creativity and beauty. Tailoring the moment to her passions will show how deeply you understand and appreciate her.

Choosing a significant holiday or special occasion can add an element of surprise and excitement to the proposal. Whether it's on her birthday, Valentine's Day, or New Year's Eve, the occasion will already be filled with love and joy, making it the ideal time to make your proposal even more memorable.

Pay attention to moments of emotional connection and shared intimacy. These instances often arise spontaneously and authentically, presenting the perfect opportunity to propose. If you both find yourselves lost in a heartfelt conversation or a tender moment, let your emotions guide you towards asking the big question.

The timing of the proposal should feel organic and natural, ensuring that it doesn't feel forced or overly scripted. Let your heart lead the way, and trust your intuition when you sense that the moment is right.

Remember that simplicity can be just as powerful as grand gestures. Sometimes, the perfect moment is a quiet and intimate one, where it's just the two of you in a cherished location, sharing your love and commitment.

Whatever moment you choose, ensure that it allows you both to be present and fully engaged in the experience. The ambiance, atmosphere, and emotional connection are what make the proposal unforgettable.

To capture the moment forever, consider enlisting the help of a photographer or videographer. Having the proposal documented allows you both to relive the magic and emotions for years to come.

Finally, be prepared for the unexpected. Life doesn't always follow a script, and the perfect moment may present itself when you least expect it. Embrace spontaneity and be flexible to seize the opportunity when it arises.

Finding the perfect moment to propose is a journey of understanding and knowing your partner deeply. By aligning the proposal with meaningful occasions, incorporating her interests, and letting your love guide you, you will create a proposal that reflects the beauty of your relationship and sets the stage for a future filled with love and happiness together. Trust in your love and commitment, and the perfect moment will unfold before you in the most extraordinary way.

Seizing the Moment: How to Discover the Ideal Time to Pop the Question"

Timing is a crucial element when it comes to proposing marriage, and seizing the perfect moment creates a proposal that is both unforgettable and deeply meaningful. Embracing spontaneity while being attuned to your partner's emotional cues will guide you towards discovering the ideal time to pop the question.

One way to seize the moment is by paying attention to your partner's reactions and emotions. Moments of genuine connection, vulnerability, and shared joy create a magical ambiance for a proposal. Observe when she is most relaxed and open, as these instances often present the perfect opportunity to express your love and commitment.

Celebrating special occasions or significant milestones in your relationship can be the ideal time to propose. Whether it's an anniversary, a meaningful date, or a shared achievement, these occasions naturally infuse the moment with sentimentality and significance.

Be open to unexpected moments that arise in your daily lives. Sometimes, the most remarkable opportunities to propose occur spontaneously. Embrace the beauty of unpredictability, and when you feel a surge of overwhelming love and affection, that may be the perfect time to pop the question.

Consider your partner's preferences and interests when planning the proposal. Whether it's her favorite season, a beloved location, or an activity she enjoys, incorporating these elements will make the proposal deeply personal and tailored to her.

A proposal doesn't have to be extravagant to be impactful. Sometimes, a simple and intimate moment, such as during a quiet evening at home or a shared adventure in nature, can hold profound meaning and create an everlasting memory.

Listen to your heart and trust your instincts. Your intuition will guide you towards the ideal moment to express your love and ask for her hand in marriage. When you feel that deep connection and an overwhelming desire to take this next step together, that's the moment to seize.

While it's essential to seize the right moment, remember that love knows no timeline. Don't feel pressured to propose on a specific date or occasion if it doesn't feel authentic to your relationship. The beauty of a proposal lies in its sincerity and the unique connection you share with your partner.

In the end, the ideal time to pop the question is when your love for each other is at its peak. By being present, attentive, and open to spontaneous possibilities, you'll discover the perfect moment to express your commitment and devotion. A proposal filled with love and genuine emotion will create a cherished memory that marks the beginning of a beautiful journey together. Trust in your love, embrace the moment, and let your heart guide you towards the most extraordinary proposal experience.

Recognizing milestone moments and shared accomplishments that signify the right time for a proposal

As your relationship deepens, reaching milestone moments and sharing accomplishments together can signify the right time for a proposal. These special occasions mark significant steps in your journey as a couple, making them ideal opportunities to pop the question and celebrate your love and commitment.

Anniversaries are one of the most classic milestone moments that signal the right time for a proposal. Whether it's your first anniversary or a milestone year, these occasions hold sentimental value and mark the growth of your relationship. Proposing on an anniversary not only celebrates the time you've spent together but also sets the stage for the exciting future ahead.

Shared accomplishments can also provide a perfect backdrop for a proposal. Achieving a major personal or professional goal as a couple signifies a strong sense of partnership and support. Celebrating these accomplishments with a proposal further cements your commitment and creates a lasting memory of your journey together.

Graduations and career advancements are moments of great achievement that can coincide with the right time to propose. These milestones represent growth and progress, making them ideal opportunities to showcase your dedication to a future built together.

If you've traveled the world together or experienced significant adventures, these shared experiences can inspire an unforgettable proposal. Whether it's atop a mountain peak you conquered together or on a beautiful beach where you found solace, proposing amidst cherished memories adds a profound layer of significance.

Shared family celebrations, such as holidays or reunions, can also serve as a perfect time to propose. Gathering with loved ones creates a warm and supportive atmosphere, providing a meaningful backdrop for your declaration of love.

Remember that each relationship is unique, and the right time for a proposal may vary for every couple. The key is to be attentive to the milestones and accomplishments you share as a couple and the emotional connections that deepen along the way.

When you feel the time is right, trust your instincts and let your heart guide you. The perfect proposal is one that is authentic, sincere, and filled with love. By recognizing milestone moments and shared accomplishments, you create a proposal that not only honors your past but also signifies a beautiful future together, hand in hand.

Creating opportunities for memorable experiences to enhance the proposal setting.

Crafting a memorable proposal setting involves more than just finding the right moment; it's about creating an experience that will be etched in your partner's heart forever. By thoughtfully planning and curating the ambiance, you can elevate your proposal and make it a cherished memory that you both treasure.

Choosing a meaningful location is the foundation of a memorable proposal setting. Consider places that hold sentimental value for your relationship, such as where you first met, shared your first date, or had a significant milestone. Proposing in a location that symbolizes your love will infuse the moment with deep emotional connections.

Embrace the beauty of nature to create a breathtaking backdrop for your proposal. Whether it's a serene beach, a picturesque park, or a scenic mountaintop, nature's splendor adds a sense of wonder and romance to the setting.

Incorporate elements of surprise to make the experience even more unforgettable. Consider arranging for a favorite musician to play a song that holds special meaning for both of you or setting up a display of photographs that capture your journey as a couple. These unexpected touches will add an element of delight and personalization to the proposal.

Timing is everything, so plan your proposal around a magical moment. Sunsets and sunrises, with their captivating hues, offer an enchanting atmosphere. The golden hour or a starlit night can also set a romantic stage for your heartfelt proposal.

Create an intimate atmosphere by considering the details. Decorate the space with fairy lights, candles, or flowers to set the mood. A cozy picnic or a private dinner under the stars can provide the perfect setting for an intimate proposal.

Consider involving loved ones, as their presence can add warmth and support to the moment. Whether it's having close family and friends nearby or inviting them to be part of the surprise, their love and encouragement will make the proposal even more meaningful.

Capture the moment with photography or videography to preserve the joy and emotions of the proposal. Having a professional or a trusted friend document the experience will allow you both to relive the magic for years to come.

Above all, let your love and genuine emotions shine through. The most memorable proposal settings are those that are filled with authenticity and sincerity. Your partner will treasure the proposal not just for the setting, but for the love and commitment you express during this special moment.

Creating opportunities for memorable experiences sets the stage for an unforgettable proposal. By infusing the setting with sentiment, surprise, and intimacy, you'll create a moment that captures the essence of your love story, one that you'll both cherish as you begin your journey towards a lifetime of happiness together.

Leveraging special occasions and holidays to add magic and significance to the proposal

Proposing on a special occasion or holiday infuses the moment with an extra dose of magic and significance. These occasions are already filled with love and joy, making them the perfect backdrop to create an unforgettable and meaningful proposal experience.

Valentine's Day, the day of love, is an ideal occasion to propose. The romantic ambiance of the day sets the stage for expressing your deepest feelings and commitment. The shared celebration of love adds an extra layer of significance to the proposal, making it a cherished memory for both of you.

Birthdays are another wonderful time to pop the question. Celebrating your partner's special day with a surprise proposal showcases your love and devotion, making the occasion even more memorable and joyous. It becomes a day she'll cherish forever, celebrating not only her birthday but also your love and future together.

New Year's Eve offers a magical moment for a proposal as you welcome a new year and new chapter in your lives. The promise of a fresh start and new beginnings adds symbolism to the proposal, making it a moment of hope and excitement for the future you'll build together.

Christmas and other holiday gatherings provide a warm and festive atmosphere for a proposal. Surrounded by loved ones and the spirit of giving, your proposal becomes a cherished family memory, embraced with love and support from those who matter most.

Consider proposing on an anniversary that holds special meaning for your relationship. Whether it's the anniversary of your first date or the day you officially became a couple, tying the proposal to this date adds sentimental value and celebrates the growth of your love over time.

If your partner has a favorite holiday, incorporating elements of that holiday into the proposal will show how much you value and appreciate her interests and passions. It adds a personal touch that makes the proposal uniquely meaningful for both of you.

No matter the occasion, remember to be genuine and sincere in your proposal. Express your love from the heart, and let the significance of the moment shine through. The magic of the occasion will amplify your emotions, making the proposal a cherished memory that you'll both carry with you as you journey into a future filled with love and happiness.

Chapter 3: Understanding Her Dream Proposal

A dream proposal is a cherished desire for many individuals, and understanding your partner's vision for this magical moment is the key to creating a proposal that reflects your love and commitment in the most meaningful way. Taking the time to discover her dream proposal will not only show how deeply you care but also create a memory that she will treasure for a lifetime.

Communication is the cornerstone of understanding her dream proposal. Engage in open and honest conversations about love, commitment, and the future. Through these discussions, gently inquire about her thoughts on marriage and proposals. Encourage her to share her dreams and aspirations, and listen attentively to what she envisions for this special moment.

Pay close attention to hints she may have dropped over time. Her reactions to other couples' proposals or her comments about what she finds romantic can provide valuable insight into her ideal proposal scenario. These clues can guide you towards crafting a proposal that aligns with her preferences and desires.

Take inspiration from her favorite movies, books, or fairytales. Often, these romantic stories offer glimpses into the types of gestures and settings she finds enchanting. While your proposal should remain authentic to your relationship, incorporating elements from her cherished stories can add a touch of magic and sentimentality.

Consider her personality and interests when envisioning her dream proposal. If she is an introverted person who values intimacy and privacy, a quiet and secluded setting may be more appealing to her. On the other hand, an extroverted individual may appreciate a grand gesture surrounded by friends and family.

Think about her favorite locations or places that hold sentimental value for your relationship. Whether it's where you had your first date, shared a special moment, or simply a place she adores, proposing in such a location can make the moment even more meaningful.

Remember that a dream proposal is not necessarily about extravagance, but about thoughtfulness and sincerity. It's about making her feel cherished, loved, and appreciated. The effort and attention you put into understanding her dream proposal will be a testament to your commitment and devotion.

Keep in mind that while understanding her dream proposal is essential, the proposal should still reflect your own personality and style as a couple. It should be an authentic expression of your love and the unique bond you share. Strive to strike a balance between her dream vision and your genuine feelings.

Once you have a clear understanding of her dream proposal, it's time to bring your vision to life. Whether it's an intimate candlelit dinner, a grand public gesture, or a romantic getaway, the key is to create an experience that will sweep her off her feet and leave her with a beautiful memory to cherish forever.

In the end, it's the love, thoughtfulness, and effort you invest in the proposal that will make it truly special. By understanding her dream proposal and infusing it with your authentic love, you'll create a moment of profound significance that will mark the beginning of a lifetime of happiness together.

Fulfilling Her Wishes: Unraveling the Mystery of Her Dream Proposal

Every person's dream proposal is as unique as the love they share, and unraveling the mystery of her dream proposal requires attentive observation and heartfelt communication. Delving into the depths of her desires and understanding her vision for this magical moment is a testament to your commitment and love.

Start by engaging in open conversations about your future together. Encourage her to share her thoughts on marriage and proposals, and express your own feelings on the matter as well. Honest and authentic communication is the foundation for understanding her wishes and desires.

Pay attention to her reactions to other proposals. Whether it's during a movie or witnessing a friend's engagement, take note of what aspects she finds particularly touching or romantic. These subtle cues can offer valuable insights into the elements she values most in a proposal.

Listen to her stories, memories, and dreams. Often, the clues to her dream proposal lie within the narratives she shares about her favorite romantic experiences or ideal scenarios. Her stories can provide a glimpse into the gestures and settings that hold a special place in her heart.

Consider her personality and interests. Think about what makes her heart skip a beat, what brings a smile to her face, and what makes her feel truly cherished. Tailoring the proposal to reflect her passions and preferences will make the moment even more meaningful and unforgettable.

Take inspiration from the little things. Pay attention to her favorite flowers, favorite foods, or activities she loves. Incorporating these small, thoughtful details into the proposal can show how deeply you know and care for her.

Consider seeking guidance from her close friends or family members. They may have valuable insights into her dream proposal or be able to offer suggestions that align with her desires.

Remember that a dream proposal is not about extravagant gestures, but about sincerity and thoughtfulness. It's about showing her that you understand and cherish her, and that your love for her is boundless.

As you unravel the mystery of her dream proposal, keep in mind that it's the genuine effort and love you put into the moment that will make it truly special. Be true to yourself as a couple, and let your love and commitment shine through in every detail.

Creating her dream proposal is a beautiful expression of your love and devotion. By understanding her wishes and desires, you'll craft a proposal that will be etched in her heart forever, a memory she'll cherish as the beginning of a lifetime of love and happiness together.

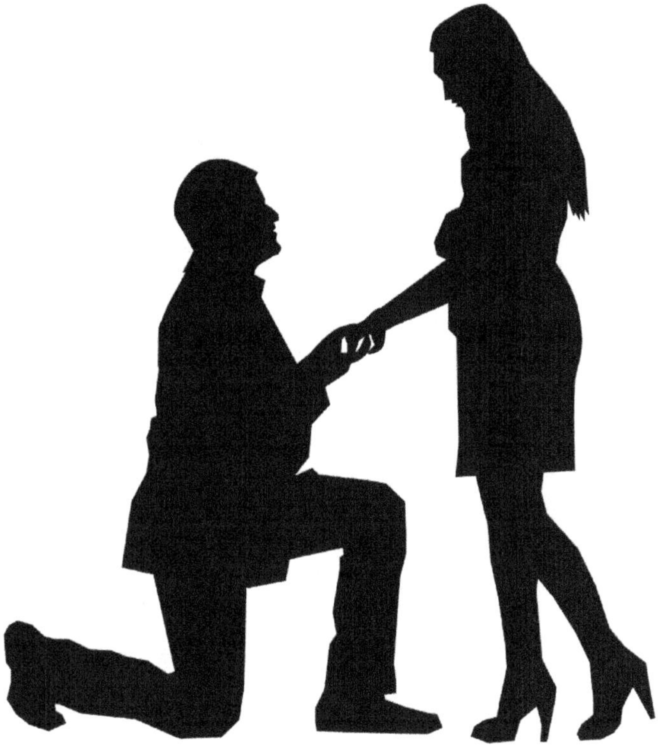

Discovering her proposal fantasies through subtle inquiries and open conversations

Unraveling the enchanting world of her proposal fantasies begins with subtle inquiries and open conversations. Delicately exploring her dreams and desires for this pivotal moment will allow you to craft a proposal that embodies the essence of your love story and fulfills her deepest wishes.

Initiate casual conversations about engagements or weddings to gauge her general thoughts and feelings on the subject. Ask about her favorite proposal stories or what elements she finds romantic in a proposal. These gentle inquiries can provide valuable insights into her proposal fantasies.

Take advantage of moments of emotional connection and vulnerability to engage in more profound conversations. Create a safe and supportive space for her to share her dreams and aspirations for the future. Encourage her to speak from the heart, and actively listen to the details she shares.

Share your own feelings about the idea of marriage and proposals to foster an environment of openness and sincerity. By expressing your own thoughts and desires, you create a mutual understanding of the significance of the moment.

Observe her reactions to romantic movies, TV shows, or real-life proposal videos. Her responses can offer glimpses into the gestures and settings that resonate with her heart.

During a date night or a leisurely walk, ask her what her dream proposal scenario would be. Encourage her to paint a picture of the perfect moment and listen attentively to her words. Let her imagination flow freely, and take note of the elements that light up her eyes.

Be attentive to hints she may drop in everyday conversations. If she admires a friend's engagement ring or expresses a fascination with a specific location, these subtle clues can guide your proposal planning.

Consider involving her close friends or family members. They may have insights into her proposal fantasies or be able to offer suggestions that align with her desires. Just ensure that they can keep the secret if you plan a surprise proposal.

Remember that discovering her proposal fantasies is not about replicating an exact scenario, but about understanding her desires and incorporating meaningful elements into the proposal. Be genuine and true to your relationship while embracing the magic of her dreams.

By embarking on subtle inquiries and open conversations, you'll unravel the tapestry of her proposal fantasies and gain precious insights into her heart's desires. The effort and thoughtfulness you put into understanding her dreams will lay the foundation for a proposal that captures the essence of your love, making it a moment she'll cherish forever.

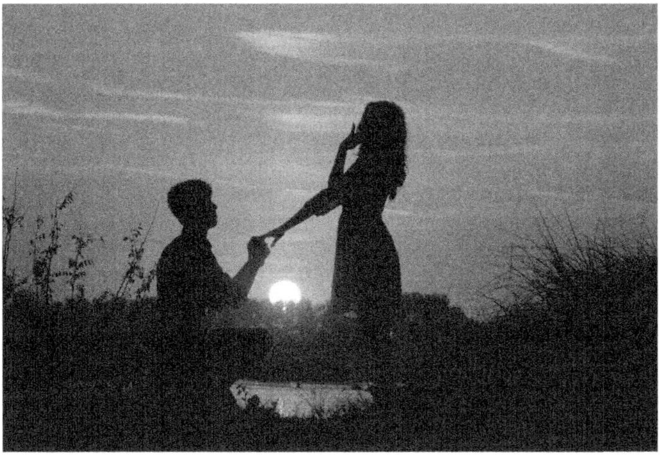

Analyzing her favorite romantic stories and movies to identify elements she desires in her proposal

The world of romantic stories and movies can offer valuable glimpses into the elements that capture her heart and desires. By carefully analyzing her favorite romantic tales, you can identify the elements she longs for in her dream proposal and craft a moment that embodies the essence of these cherished narratives.

Pay attention to the type of romantic stories and movies she enjoys. Whether it's classic love stories, whimsical fairytales, or contemporary romances, each genre can provide clues to her preferences and fantasies.

Notice the settings that feature prominently in her favorite romantic tales. Whether it's a magical castle, a serene beach, or a bustling cityscape, the locations depicted can give insight into the atmosphere she finds most enchanting.

Look for recurring themes in these stories. Whether it's a grand gesture of love, an intimate moment of vulnerability, or a declaration of lifelong commitment, these themes may mirror her desires for her own proposal.

Observe the gestures and actions of the characters that resonate with her. Whether it's a heartfelt love letter, a surprise candlelit dinner, or a romantic dance under the stars, these gestures can offer inspiration for your proposal planning.

Pay attention to the emotions evoked by these stories. Whether they elicit tears of joy or warm smiles, the emotions stirred by her favorite romantic tales can offer a glimpse into the feelings she hopes to experience during her own proposal.

Consider the symbolism and motifs portrayed in these stories. Whether it's a specific flower, a meaningful piece of jewelry, or a shared activity, these symbols may hold sentimental value for her, making them meaningful elements to incorporate into the proposal.

Engage in discussions about her favorite romantic stories and movies. Ask her what elements she finds particularly romantic or what moments resonate with her the most. Encourage her to share her thoughts and feelings, and listen attentively to her responses.

While analyzing her favorite romantic tales can offer valuable insights, remember that the proposal should still reflect your unique love story as a couple. Infuse your proposal with genuine emotions and personal touches that speak to your relationship.

By understanding the elements she desires in her dream proposal through her favorite romantic stories and movies, you'll be equipped to craft a moment that captures the essence of her fantasies. The effort and thoughtfulness you put into creating this magical experience will be a testament to your love and commitment, making it a proposal she'll cherish as the beginning of your beautiful journey together.

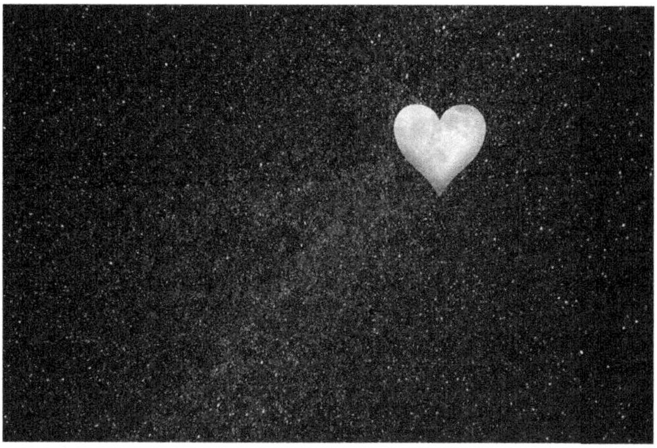

Paying attention to her reactions to others' proposals to discern her preferences.

One of the most telling ways to understand her proposal preferences is by observing her reactions to others' proposals. Whether it's in movies, TV shows, or witnessing real-life engagements, her responses can provide valuable insights into the elements that resonate with her heart.

Watch her facial expressions and body language when she witnesses a proposal. Does she light up with joy and excitement, or does she seem moved to tears? Her emotional response can indicate the gestures and settings that deeply touch her.

Listen to her comments and remarks after witnessing a proposal. Does she express admiration for certain aspects, such as the location, the surprise element, or the sentiment behind the proposal? Her verbal cues can offer valuable clues about the elements she finds meaningful.

Notice if she initiates conversations about proposal stories or shares engagement announcements with enthusiasm. This eagerness to discuss proposals may signify her own thoughts and desires on the subject.

Consider the moments she rewatches or discusses with friends and family. If certain proposal scenes or stories hold a special place in her heart, it's likely they align with her dreams for her own proposal.

Be attentive to any ideas or suggestions she drops during casual conversations about engagements or weddings. Whether she mentions her favorite flowers, a dream destination, or a unique idea for a proposal, these subtle hints can guide your planning.

Engage in open conversations about the proposals she witnesses. Ask her what elements she finds romantic or touching in those moments. Encourage her to share her thoughts and feelings, and listen attentively to her responses.

Remember that every person's proposal preferences are unique, so avoid making assumptions based solely on others' proposals. Use these observations as a starting point to understand her desires, but let her personality and preferences guide your final decision.

Ultimately, the most meaningful proposal will be one that aligns with your relationship and showcases your genuine love and commitment. By paying attention to her reactions to others' proposals, you'll gain valuable insights into the elements she finds enchanting, allowing you to create a proposal that will be a cherished memory she holds close to her heart.

Chapter 4: Unconventional and Personalized Approaches

In a world filled with love stories, creating an unconventional and personalized proposal allows you to showcase the distinctive bond you share as a couple. By daring to be different and infusing your authentic selves into the moment, you can craft a proposal that becomes a beautiful reflection of your love story, leaving an indelible mark on both of your hearts.

Consider her passions and interests as a starting point for an unconventional proposal. Whether she loves art, music, sports, or any other hobby, incorporating her passions into the proposal can add a touch of personalization and creativity. For example, you could organize an art exhibit with paintings depicting your love story or arrange a surprise performance of her favorite song with personalized lyrics.

Embrace the beauty of nature for a unique proposal setting. A scenic hike to a breathtaking viewpoint, a hot air balloon ride with panoramic views, or a tranquil camping trip under the stars can create an unforgettable backdrop for the moment you pop the question.

Make technology work in your favor. In today's digital age, you can take advantage of virtual reality or augmented reality to create an innovative and immersive proposal experience. Imagine proposing in a virtual world that holds special meaning for both of you or using AR to reveal hidden messages leading to the proposal spot.

Celebrate your shared interests and sense of adventure with an unconventional proposal idea. If you both love traveling, consider proposing during a surprise trip to a bucket-list destination. For thrill-seekers, an adrenaline-pumping activity like skydiving or bungee jumping can make the proposal unforgettable.

Incorporate nostalgia and sentimental moments to add a personal touch. Revisit the place where you first met or had your first date, or recreate a cherished memory from earlier in your relationship. These nostalgic gestures will evoke heartfelt emotions and show how much those moments still mean to both of you.

Involve friends, family, or even your pets to create an intimate and heartwarming proposal. A flash mob of loved ones performing a dance, or your furry friends walking down the aisle with the engagement ring, can make the proposal even more memorable and meaningful.

Think outside the box for the actual proposal method. Instead of a traditional down-on-one-knee approach, consider a puzzle proposal where she unravels a riddle or a scavenger hunt leading to the question. Or create a personalized book that narrates your love story, culminating in the proposal on the final page.

Unconventional proposals don't have to be extravagant or over-the-top; they simply need to resonate with your relationship and your personalities as a couple. The key is to make it personal, thoughtful, and true to who you are.

By embracing unconventional and personalized approaches, you showcase the uniqueness of your love, creating a proposal that will stand out as a beautiful representation of your journey together. It will be a moment etched in your hearts forever, reminding you both of the depth of your love and the joyous adventure you embarked on when you said "yes" to forever.

Beyond Tradition: Crafting Unique and Personal Proposals She'll Never Forget

When it comes to proposing, going beyond tradition and creating a unique and personal experience is an opportunity to make a lasting impression on your partner. By infusing your proposal with elements that hold significance for your relationship, you can craft a moment she'll cherish forever.

Start by reflecting on your journey together. Think about the moments that defined your love story, the inside jokes, shared adventures, and the experiences that strengthened your bond. Incorporate these personal touches into the proposal to make it a celebration of your unique connection.

Consider her interests and passions as a guiding inspiration. Whether it's a favorite hobby, a cherished destination, or a specific artistic style, incorporating elements that hold special meaning for her will show how deeply you know and cherish her.

Think about your partner's personality and preferences. Is she someone who loves surprises and grand gestures, or does she appreciate intimate and heartfelt moments? Tailoring the proposal to align with her preferences will make it all the more meaningful.

Create a proposal that tells your love story. From a heartfelt letter chronicling your journey together to a personalized video showcasing your shared memories, incorporating these elements will make the proposal deeply sentimental and unforgettable.

Choose an unconventional location or setting to add an element of surprise and excitement. Whether it's a beautiful rooftop, a secluded beach, or a charming garden, the setting can create an enchanting ambiance for the moment you ask her to be yours forever.

Involve loved ones or furry friends in the proposal to make it a heartwarming and joyful experience. The support and love of family and friends can add an extra layer of significance to the moment.

Consider incorporating a unique ritual or tradition from your cultures or backgrounds. Celebrating your heritage in the proposal will make it a beautiful representation of your shared identities.

Whether it's a romantic scavenger hunt leading to the proposal spot or a surprise serenade under the stars, the key is to be thoughtful, genuine, and true to your relationship. By crafting a unique and personal proposal, you demonstrate the depth of your love and commitment, making it a moment she'll treasure forever in her heart. Beyond tradition lies the magic of creating an experience that celebrates your love story in a way that's uniquely yours.

Exploring non-traditional proposal ideas that align with her interests and passions

When it comes to proposing, exploring non-traditional ideas that align with her interests and passions can elevate the moment to something truly extraordinary. By infusing elements that resonate with her on a personal level, you create a proposal that reflects the depth of your understanding and love for her.

Consider her hobbies and passions as a starting point for a non-traditional proposal. Whether she loves art, music, literature, sports, or any other pursuit, incorporating these interests into the proposal will show how much you value and support her passions.

Plan an adventure proposal that aligns with her sense of wanderlust and love for exploration. Whether it's a surprise trip to a dream destination or a thrilling outdoor activity she enjoys, the excitement and sense of discovery will make the proposal unforgettable.

For the food enthusiast, consider proposing during a private cooking class or a romantic dinner at her favorite restaurant. Sharing a meal created with love will add a touch of intimacy and personalization to the moment.

If she enjoys the arts, create a proposal that celebrates creativity and beauty. Organize an art exhibit featuring her favorite artists or propose during a live performance of her beloved musician or theater production.

For the nature lover, plan a proposal in the great outdoors. Whether it's a hike to a breathtaking view, a cozy campfire under the stars, or a peaceful picnic in a scenic garden, the beauty of nature will enhance the romance of the moment.

Consider involving animals in the proposal if she has a soft spot for furry friends. A surprise visit to an animal sanctuary or proposing with the help of your pets can add a heartwarming and joyful element to the experience.

Personalize the proposal with custom-made elements that reflect your relationship. From a handcrafted engagement ring designed with her favorite gemstone to a song you wrote that tells your love story, these personalized touches will make the proposal deeply sentimental.

Plan a proposal that aligns with her values and beliefs. Whether it's a charitable event that supports a cause close to her heart or a sustainable and eco-friendly celebration, incorporating these aspects will show your respect for her principles.

Remember that a non-traditional proposal doesn't mean deviating from the essence of love and commitment. Instead, it's about tailoring the moment to her passions and interests, creating an experience that celebrates your unique connection and shared journey.

By exploring non-traditional proposal ideas that align with her interests and passions, you demonstrate your thoughtfulness and genuine understanding of her as an individual. The effort you put into crafting a proposal that celebrates her will make the moment truly special and a cherished memory she'll carry with her as you embark on a future filled with love and happiness together

.Incorporating shared hobbies, inside jokes, and cherished memories into the proposal plan

The most meaningful and unforgettable proposals often come from weaving the tapestry of your unique love story into the moment. By incorporating shared hobbies, inside jokes, and cherished memories, you create a proposal plan that celebrates the essence of your relationship and showcases your profound connection.

Begin by reflecting on the hobbies and activities that bring you both joy and draw you closer together. Whether it's cooking, hiking, painting, or dancing, integrating these shared hobbies into the proposal plan will make the moment feel authentically "you." For instance, if you both love cooking, consider organizing a surprise cooking class followed by a romantic dinner where you pop the question.

Inside jokes are intimate treasures that only you two share. Including them in the proposal plan will bring laughter and joy to the moment. Whether it's referencing a funny moment from your first date or a beloved catchphrase, these inside jokes will add a touch of lightness and familiarity to the proposal.

Cherished memories hold sentimental value in your journey as a couple. Incorporate them into the proposal to evoke heartfelt emotions and create a profound connection. Revisiting the place where you had your first date or recreating a special moment from your past will remind both of you of the depth of your love.

Personalize the proposal plan with elements that speak to your relationship. If you have a favorite song that encapsulates your love story, arrange for a musician to serenade you both before the proposal. Or create a photo album filled with snapshots of your cherished memories, culminating in the last page with the question "Will you marry me?"

Remember that the beauty of incorporating shared hobbies, inside jokes, and cherished memories into the proposal plan lies in the intimacy and sincerity of the moment. By doing so, you show your partner that you truly know and cherish her, making the proposal a reflection of your profound bond.

Crafting a proposal filled with heartfelt meaning not only creates a lasting memory but also sets the stage for a future built on love and shared experiences. By incorporating the essence of your relationship into the proposal plan, you create a moment that celebrates your unique connection, reminding both of you of the beautiful journey you've embarked upon together.

Embracing creativity and thinking outside the box to make the proposal one-of-a-kind

Embracing Creativity and Thinking Outside the Box: Crafting a One-of-a-Kind Proposal

When it comes to proposing, embracing creativity and thinking outside the box can transform a special moment into a truly extraordinary and one-of-a-kind experience. By infusing your proposal with unique elements and unexpected surprises, you create a memory that will forever be etched in your partner's heart.

Start by brainstorming ideas that are unconventional and personalized to your relationship. Think about what sets your love story apart and what makes your bond special. Consider your partner's interests, passions, and favorite things, and use them as a foundation for your creative proposal.

Go beyond traditional settings and explore unique locations that hold significance for your relationship. Whether it's a hidden gem in nature, a quirky urban spot, or a place that sparked a meaningful conversation, choosing an unconventional location can add a sense of adventure and intimacy to the proposal.

Incorporate interactive elements that engage your partner in the proposal. Consider creating a scavenger hunt leading to different places that hold memories for both of you, or involve her in a fun activity that culminates in the proposal moment. These interactive experiences will make the proposal even more memorable and enjoyable.

Enlist the help of family and friends to add an element of surprise and joy. Whether it's through a flash mob, a heartfelt video message, or a surprise guest appearance, involving loved ones in the proposal will create a sense of community and support during this special moment.

Think about incorporating technology and innovative ideas. From creating a personalized app or website that leads to the proposal to using virtual reality to create a unique proposal setting, technology can elevate the experience and add a touch of modernity to the moment.

Consider unexpected and magical elements that will leave your partner in awe. Whether it's releasing lanterns into the night sky, arranging a surprise fireworks display, or hiring a professional performer, these touches will add a sense of enchantment and romance to the proposal.

Remember that the key to a one-of-a-kind proposal is authenticity and staying true to your relationship. Embrace creativity and think outside the box while infusing the proposal with your genuine love and heartfelt emotions.

By embracing creativity and thinking outside the box, you create a proposal that captures the essence of your love story in a way that's uniquely yours. This unforgettable moment will be a testament to your commitment and devotion, setting the stage for a future filled with love and cherished memories together.

Chapter 5: Enlisting Help and Making It Memorable

Proposing is a momentous occasion, and enlisting help and making it memorable can turn this significant moment into a cherished memory that you both will treasure forever. By involving loved ones, planning unique surprises, and creating a thoughtful atmosphere, you can make your proposal truly unforgettable.

1. Involve Loved Ones: Enlisting the support of family and close friends can add warmth and joy to the proposal. Consider organizing a gathering with your loved ones present to witness the proposal or even help with the surprise. Their presence and encouragement will make the moment even more meaningful.

2. Capture the Moment: Hiring a professional photographer or videographer to discreetly capture the proposal will allow you to relive the magic in vivid detail. The photos and videos will become cherished mementos, preserving the emotions and reactions from this special day.

3. Create a Sentimental Timeline: Plan a journey that showcases the significant moments of your relationship. Take her on a romantic stroll through the places where you first met, had your first date, or shared cherished memories. End the journey with the proposal, adding a layer of sentimentality to the moment.

4. Tailor It to Her Interests: Craft the proposal around her hobbies and passions. Whether it's incorporating her favorite flower, book, or movie into the setting, or planning an activity she loves, aligning the proposal with her interests will show how much you care.

5. Surprise Getaway: Plan a surprise weekend getaway to a destination that holds sentimental value or has been on her bucket list. The element of surprise and the excitement of exploring a new place together will create a memorable backdrop for the proposal.

6. Personalize the Ring: If possible, consider designing a custom engagement ring that reflects her style and personality. A ring that speaks to her taste and preferences will make the moment even more special.

7. Thoughtful Gestures: Small, thoughtful gestures can add a personal touch to the proposal. Write her a heartfelt letter or create a personalized gift that celebrates your relationship. These heartfelt touches will showcase your love and dedication.

8. Surprise Party: If she loves surprises and being surrounded by loved ones, consider organizing a surprise proposal party. Invite friends and family to celebrate the occasion with you after the proposal.

9. A Touch of Nostalgia: Bring nostalgia into the proposal by incorporating elements from your early dating days or revisiting places where you had significant moments together. Reliving those cherished memories will add a layer of sentimentality to the proposal.

10. Plan a Treasure Hunt: Organize a scavenger hunt with clues leading to different locations that are special to your relationship. At the final destination, you can be waiting to pop the question, making the proposal an exciting adventure.

Remember that the most memorable proposals are those that reflect your love and commitment as a couple. Tailor the proposal to her preferences, and let your genuine emotions shine through. By enlisting help and making it memorable, you create a proposal that celebrates your unique love story and marks the beginning of a beautiful journey together.

The Power of Teamwork: Enlisting Support for a Heartwarming and Unforgettable Proposal

Proposing to the love of your life is a moment filled with love, excitement, and anticipation. To create a heartwarming and unforgettable proposal, consider harnessing the power of teamwork by enlisting the support of others. Involving family, friends, or even strangers can add an extra layer of magic and meaning to this significant moment in your lives.

1. Family and Friends: Your closest family members and friends are your biggest cheerleaders, and their presence and support can make the proposal even more heartwarming. Consider organizing a small gathering with your loved ones, where you can propose in the midst of those who mean the most to you both. Their smiles, tears of joy, and heartfelt applause will create a treasured memory.

2. Capturing the Moment: Hiring a professional photographer or videographer can ensure that the precious moments of the proposal are beautifully preserved. Candid shots of the

proposal and the genuine reactions of your partner and loved ones will become cherished keepsakes that you can revisit time and time again.

3. Public Engagement: If your partner loves being in the spotlight, consider proposing in a public setting, such as a favorite park or a busy city square. Enlist the help of a street performer or a flash mob to create a heartwarming surprise that will leave her beaming with happiness.

4. Pet Partners: If you share a beloved pet, consider incorporating them into the proposal. Pets are family, too, and involving them in the moment will add an adorable and heartwarming touch to the proposal.

5. Musical Serenade: Music has a magical way of evoking emotions and setting the tone for special moments. Arrange for a musician or a group of singers to perform your partner's favorite song or a song that holds special meaning for your relationship. The heartfelt melody will create an emotional and unforgettable ambiance.

6. Social Media Surprise: If your partner is active on social media, consider a creative way to propose online. Share a heartfelt post, a video, or a series of pictures that lead to the final question. The well-wishes and messages of love from friends and family will make the proposal even more heartwarming.

7. Memory Lane: Take your partner on a journey down memory lane by revisiting places where you had significant moments in your relationship. Each location can hold a clue or a small token that leads to the next stop, culminating in the proposal destination.

8. Cultural Celebration: If you and your partner come from different cultural backgrounds, consider incorporating elements from both cultures into the proposal. Embracing each other's heritage will make the proposal a celebration of your unique identities and shared love.

9. A Community of Strangers: Sometimes, the kindness of strangers can play a significant role in creating heartwarming proposals. Reach out to people in public spaces, such as a beach or a

park, to be part of a surprise proposal scene. The willingness of others to join in will leave a lasting impact on both of you.

10. Create a Video Tribute: Gather heartfelt video messages from friends and family expressing their love and support for your relationship. Compile these messages into a heartwarming video montage that you can play before popping the question.

Remember, the power of teamwork lies in the shared love and support that surround you both. By enlisting the help of others, you create a heartwarming and unforgettable proposal that celebrates the love you share and the beautiful journey that lies ahead. It's a moment that will forever be etched in your hearts, a testament to the power of love and the strength of your relationships with those who matter most.

Involving friends and family to create a surprise-filled proposal that showcases your love and support system

Incorporating friends and family into your proposal can transform this special moment into a heartwarming and surprise-filled celebration of your love and support system. The involvement of your loved ones adds an extra layer of joy and meaning, making the proposal a memory that you and your partner will treasure forever.

Enlisting the help of friends and family allows you to create a surprise-filled proposal that keeps your partner on her toes. From planning a covert surprise party to organizing a flash mob, their collaboration adds an element of excitement and unpredictability to the moment.

Including loved ones in the proposal showcases the strength of your support system. Your partner will be deeply touched to see the important people in your life coming together to witness and celebrate your love. It reinforces the idea that you both are surrounded by a loving community that cherishes your relationship.

Involving friends and family is an opportunity to honor and acknowledge the significant roles they play in your lives. Their presence and participation in the proposal will create a shared memory that bonds all of you together in the celebration of love.

Your loved ones can offer valuable support and creative ideas for the proposal planning. They know you and your partner well, and their insights can help you tailor the proposal to your partner's preferences and create a moment that truly represents your unique love story.

Additionally, having friends and family by your side during the proposal can ease any nervousness you may have. Their encouragement and reassurance will give you the confidence to express your love and make the proposal even more heartfelt.

The involvement of friends and family also allows you to capture the proposal from different perspectives. Their candid reactions and emotional expressions will become cherished memories captured in photos and videos that you can revisit time and time again.

Remember to carefully coordinate with your loved ones to ensure that the proposal remains a surprise for your partner. Communicate with them about the plan and timing to maintain the element of astonishment.

In conclusion, involving friends and family in your proposal creates a surprise-filled and heartwarming celebration of your love and support system. Their presence adds joy and meaning to the moment, making it a cherished memory for you, your partner, and all those who share in your happiness. It showcases the strength of your relationships and reinforces the beautiful journey you are embarking upon together.

Hiring professionals, such as photographers or musicians, to capture the moment and enhance the experience

When planning a proposal, hiring professionals, such as photographers or musicians, can elevate the moment and make it even more special. These skilled individuals can help capture the emotions and reactions, ensuring that the proposal becomes a treasured memory for a lifetime.

Photographers play a crucial role in immortalizing the proposal. By hiring a professional photographer, you can focus on the moment itself while knowing that every heartfelt reaction and joyous expression will be beautifully captured. The photographs will serve as a tangible reminder of the love and excitement shared during the proposal.

Videographers offer another layer of depth to the experience. A professionally filmed video will capture the sights, sounds, and emotions of the proposal, allowing you both to relive the magic over and over again. The video becomes a heartfelt keepsake, preserving not only the proposal but also the love and joy surrounding it.

Musicians can add a touch of romance and ambiance to the proposal. Whether it's a solo musician playing your partner's favorite song or a small ensemble creating a harmonious melody, live music creates an emotional and unforgettable atmosphere.

The expertise of these professionals can also enhance the overall experience. They can provide valuable advice on the best angles and lighting for photographs, the perfect timing for music to heighten the emotion, and even assist in choosing the ideal proposal location.

Having professionals involved allows you to be fully present in the moment. Instead of worrying about capturing the perfect shot or ensuring the music plays at the right time, you can focus on expressing your love and commitment to your partner.

Furthermore, the involvement of professionals adds a touch of luxury and thoughtfulness to the proposal. It demonstrates that you took the time and effort to curate a truly special and unforgettable experience for your partner.

Before hiring professionals, ensure that they understand your vision for the proposal and are aligned with your preferences. Choose individuals who are experienced in capturing heartfelt moments or creating an enchanting ambiance.

In conclusion, hiring professionals such as photographers or musicians can enhance the proposal experience in countless ways. They ensure that the emotions and reactions are beautifully captured, creating treasured memories that you can cherish for a lifetime. Their expertise adds an element of luxury and thoughtfulness to the proposal, demonstrating your commitment to making the moment truly special. With their support, you can focus on expressing your love and creating a heartfelt experience that will be etched in your hearts forever.

Incorporating small gestures of thoughtfulness to ensure the proposal is memorable and tailored to her preferences

When planning a proposal, it's the small gestures of thoughtfulness that can transform the moment into an unforgettable experience tailored to your partner's preferences. By paying attention to the little details and showcasing your deep understanding of her, you create a proposal that truly captures the essence of your love.

Listen and Observe: Pay attention to the things your partner loves, whether it's a favorite flower, a special place, or a cherished memory. Observing her reactions to certain experiences or objects can give you valuable clues about what will resonate with her heart during the proposal.

Personalized Proposal Setting: Choose a proposal location that holds significance in your relationship. It could be the place where you first met, had your first date, or shared a special moment together. The sentimental value of the location will make the proposal even more heartfelt.

Tailor the Proposal Speech: Craft your proposal speech to reflect your shared journey as a couple. Share heartfelt memories, future aspirations, and what makes your love unique. Your words should be a genuine expression of your feelings for her.

Incorporate Shared Interests: Infuse the proposal with elements that reflect your shared interests and hobbies. Whether it's a surprise activity you both enjoy or a small gift related to her favorite pastime, these personalized touches will show how much you value your connection.

Embrace Sentimental Keepsakes: Consider incorporating sentimental keepsakes, such as a letter, a photo album, or a custom piece of jewelry, into the proposal. These thoughtful touches will add a layer of emotion and make the moment even more unforgettable.

Involve Loved Ones: If your partner is close to her family or friends, consider involving them in the proposal. Their presence and support will make the moment even more heartwarming and significant.

Capture the Moment: Arrange for a photographer or videographer to discreetly capture the proposal. The candid shots or video will preserve the raw emotions and reactions, allowing you both to relive the magic for years to come.

Choose the Perfect Ring: Take the time to select an engagement ring that reflects her style and preferences. Consider the metal, gemstone, and design that she adores, ensuring that the ring is a symbol of your love and commitment, tailored to her taste.

By incorporating these small gestures of thoughtfulness, you show your partner that you cherish and understand her deeply. The personalized elements and sentimental touches will make the proposal an authentic representation of your love story. It's these heartfelt details that turn a simple question into a cherished memory, a proposal that she'll treasure in her heart forever.

25 of the best and most Creative way to pop the question

1. Time Capsule Surprise: Create a time capsule together and include a letter expressing your love and desire to marry her. Bury it together in a meaningful spot, and when the time is right, unearth the capsule and propose.

2. Love Lock Bridge: Take her to a famous love lock bridge or a location with a similar concept. Bring a custom padlock engraved with your names and the proposal date, and together, lock it onto the bridge.

3. Proposal Piñata: Fill a piñata with confetti, small gifts, and a heartfelt letter expressing your love. Blindfold her and have her break the piñata, revealing the proposal message and the ring.

4. Puzzle of Love: Create a custom puzzle with an image of both of you together. As she completes the puzzle, the proposal message will be revealed.

5. Enchanted Forest Proposal: Take her on a magical walk through a beautifully decorated forest or garden, with fairy lights and candles leading the way to your proposal spot.

6. Adventure Book Proposal: Create a scrapbook or adventure book detailing your relationship journey, with the last page being your proposal message.

7. Romantic Boat Ride: Arrange a private boat ride, decorate it with fairy lights and candles, and propose as you cruise under the stars.

8. Sky Lanterns Proposal: Light up the night sky with sky lanterns. Each lantern could represent a shared memory or dream, and when she releases her lantern, it will reveal the proposal.

9. Firework Show Proposal: Coordinate with a fireworks display team to create a dazzling show ending with "Will You Marry Me?" written in the sky.

10. Dance Proposal: Plan a surprise flash mob or choreographed dance routine, ending with your proposal in the spotlight.

11. Digital Proposal: Create a website or slideshow showcasing your relationship journey and proposal message, and send her the link to discover.

12. Message in a Bottle 2.0: Send her on a romantic beach walk, and have a message in a bottle waiting for her, containing your proposal letter.

13. Magical Mirror Proposal: Write your proposal message on a mirror, decorate it with fairy lights, and surprise her when she looks into the mirror.

14. Adventure Quest: Organize an adventurous quest with different challenges and clues leading to the final proposal destination.

15. Proposal in a Hot Air Balloon Basket: Arrange for the proposal message to be displayed inside the hot air balloon basket, revealing it as you both ascend.

16. Retro Movie Theater Proposal: Rent a vintage movie theater and screen a custom-made movie of your love story, ending with the proposal.

17. Star Naming Proposal: Name a star after her, and during a romantic stargazing night, present her with a star certificate and propose.

18. Personalized Fortune Cookies: Order custom fortune cookies with your proposal message inside and enjoy them together for a delightful surprise.

19. Proposal Underwater: If she loves the ocean, propose while snorkeling or scuba diving, with a waterproof sign or message underwater.

20. Proposal at a Wine Tasting: Plan a wine tasting event with her favorite wines, and during the tasting, have the sommelier present the engagement ring.

21. Virtual Reality Proposal: Set up a virtual reality experience with a custom proposal game or message for a modern and immersive proposal.

22. Proposal at a Favorite Childhood Spot: Take her back to a place from her childhood that holds special memories, and propose there with a heartfelt letter.

23. Photobooth Proposal: Arrange a photobooth session together, and as the final photo is taken, drop down on one knee for the proposal.

24. Sandcastle Proposal: Build a sandcastle together at the beach, and secretly place the engagement ring on top before showing her your creation.

25. Proposal Through a Romantic Song: Compose a song or perform her favorite love song with customized lyrics, ending with your proposal.

The most important element in any proposal is genuine love and thoughtfulness. Choose an idea that resonates with your girlfriend's interests and personality, and make the moment memorable and special for both of you. Best of luck on your proposal journey!

Conclusion: Embracing the Journey of Love

In the beautiful journey of love, the proposal marks a significant milestone—a moment when two souls come together to embark on a lifelong adventure filled with joy, challenges, and unconditional affection. Throughout this guide, we have explored various ways to craft a proposal that is not only unforgettable but also deeply meaningful and tailored to your partner's preferences. From understanding her dreams and desires to involving loved ones and professionals, each element contributes to creating a magical and heartfelt experience.

Remember that a proposal is not just a question; it is a declaration of love and a promise to stand by each other through life's highs and lows. Embracing the journey of love means cherishing the moments that brought you together, and celebrating the future you'll build as a team.

Your partner is unique, and so is your love story. Whether you choose an adventurous outdoor proposal, a heartfelt intimate moment, or a grand surprise with loved ones, the key is to make it personal and genuine. Tailor the proposal to reflect the essence of your relationship and the things that make your connection special.

Throughout the process, communication and observation are your allies. Pay attention to her preferences, listen to her dreams, and notice the moments that make her heart sing. Enlisting the support of friends and family can add depth and joy to the proposal, while professionals can help preserve the magic for years to come.

It's essential to trust your heart and be present in the moment. Embrace any nervousness or excitement, knowing that what truly matters is the love you share. A heartfelt proposal, filled with love and sincerity, will always be a cherished memory, no matter how simple or elaborate the execution.

Lastly, as you embrace the journey of love, remember that the proposal is just the beginning. It is the stepping stone to a life filled with shared experiences, laughter, tears, and growth together. Each day will be an opportunity to strengthen your bond and create new memories.

In the end, love is a journey that continues to unfold, and the proposal is one of the first steps on this path. Embrace the adventure with an open heart and a willingness to cherish every moment, for love is a wondrous journey that enriches our lives in ways we can never imagine.

As you move forward, may your love be a guiding light that illuminates your path, and may your commitment to each other be a source of strength and comfort in the face of any challenge. Embrace the journey of love with all its twists and turns, for it is a journey worth taking with the one who holds the key to your heart.

Printed in Great Britain
by Amazon